Shopping Addiction

Mastering Your Money
and Spending Habits

Ghazwan Alemara

Copyright © 2024 Ghazwan Alemara. All rights reserved.

No part of this publication may be reproduced, distributed, or transmitted in any form or by any means, including photocopying, recording, or other electronic or mechanical methods, without the prior written permission of the publisher, except in the case of brief quotations embodied in critical reviews and certain other noncommercial uses permitted by copyright law.

For permissions requests or inquiries, please contact the publisher at hello@ghazwan.pro

Published by ghazwan.pro.

I believe knowledge should be accessible to everyone, so I'm offering the eBook format free to all readers. To get the free copy, **scan** or **click** the QR code below.

Contents

Contents iv
Introduction 1

   Chapter 1 5
Understanding Shopping Addiction 5
   What Is Shopping Addiction? 5
   Signs of Shopping Addiction 8
   The Science Behind It 11

   Chapter 2 14
Why Do We Shop? 14
   Emotional Triggers and Shopping 14
   The Influence of Consumer Culture 17
   The Retail Therapy Myth 20

   Chapter 3 23
Breaking the Cycle 23
   Recognizing Your Triggers 23
   Mindfulness and Emotional Regulation 25
   Building Self-Awareness 28

   Chapter 4 31
Reclaiming Financial Control 31

Assessing the Damage 31
Creating a Realistic Budget 33
Debt Recovery Strategies 36

Chapter 5 40
Practical Strategies to Stop Shopping 40
How to Control Shopping Impulses 40
Establishing New Habits 43
Managing Online Shopping 46
How Well Do You Manage Your Shopping Habits? 49

Chapter 6 50
Emotional Healing and Recovery 50
Addressing the Root Causes 50
Cognitive Behavioral Techniques (CBT) 52
The Role of Therapy and Support Groups 55

Chapter 7 58
Long-Term Maintenance and Building Financial Freedom .. 58
Staying on Track 58
Building Healthy Financial Habits 60
Relapse Prevention 63

Chapter 8 67
The Digital Age and Shopping Addiction 67
Online Shopping vs. In-Store Shopping 67

    The Allure of Convenience 70
    Tools to Manage Online Shopping 72

Chapter 9 76
Success Stories and Lessons Learned 76
    Real-Life Success Stories 76
    Lessons from the Journey 79
    Your Path Forward 82
Conclusion 85

Introduction

Do you ever find yourself standing in a store aisle, holding a product you don't really need, yet something inside pushes you to buy it? Or maybe it's the thrill of placing another item in your online cart, followed by the excitement when it finally arrives at your door. For many, shopping isn't just about acquiring what we need; it has become an emotional escape, a habit that leads to overspending, debt, and guilt. But the real question is: how did we get here? And more importantly, how do we break free?

Shopping addiction is a real issue that affects more people than we realize. In today's world, with the convenience of online shopping and constant sales, the temptation to spend is always just a click away. What starts as a harmless purchase can evolve into compulsive behavior that takes control of our lives, finances, and well-being. This book is here to help you understand that cycle and, more importantly, how to break it.

Why This Book?

The goal of this book is simple: to equip you with the tools and insights needed to master your money and spending habits, breaking free from the grip of compulsive shopping.

Shopping addiction, like any other form of addiction, thrives on secrecy and isolation. Many people feel embarrassed, ashamed, or even unaware of the extent of their problem. This book will guide you in confronting it with practical advice, emotional support, and effective strategies for the real world.

Whether you have already recognized your addiction or are just starting to question your relationship with shopping, this book is designed to help you through the process of change, from understanding the causes to taking actionable steps toward recovery.

The Importance of This Journey

Shopping addiction is more than just overspending; it's often tied to deeper issues such as emotions, identity, and even mental health. In today's consumer-driven culture, people shop not just to fill their closets, but to fill emotional voids. Shopping becomes a way to cope with stress, anxiety, and even depression. Unfortunately, the short-term relief is quickly replaced by more emotional and financial strain.

In recent years, the rise of online shopping has made it easier than ever to give in to compulsive spending. With the pandemic accelerating the shift to digital, millions have developed habits of mindless shopping. This book offers timely guidance for those seeking to regain control of their spending habits and reshape their financial futures.

What You Can Expect

Throughout the chapters, this book will take you through a comprehensive approach to mastering your money and spending habits. We will start by exploring the psychology of shopping addiction: why we buy, the emotions that drive us, and how consumer culture plays a role. From there, we will dive into practical tools for breaking free, such as recognizing triggers, building healthier habits, and regaining financial control.

You'll find actionable strategies, including how to create realistic budgets, manage debt, and prevent relapse. This book is practical and grounded in real-world advice that you can apply immediately, regardless of where you are on your journey. It is also focused on emotional healing, helping you understand the reasons behind your behavior and find healthier ways to cope with life's challenges.

A Path Forward

Breaking free from shopping addiction isn't easy, but it's possible. The fact that you're reading this book means you're already on the right path. By the end of this journey, you'll have the knowledge and confidence to not only manage your finances, but also reshape your relationship with shopping and consumption. This isn't just about spending less; it's about gaining more control, more peace, and more freedom.

Let's begin this journey together, and take back control of your life, one step at a time.

Chapter 1

Understanding Shopping Addiction

What Is Shopping Addiction?

Shopping addiction, also known as compulsive buying disorder, is a behavioral addiction that goes beyond the occasional shopping spree or retail therapy. It's the overwhelming urge to buy items, even when they aren't needed or affordable, to the point where the behavior begins to negatively affect a person's life. Like any other addiction, shopping addiction isn't about the thing being consumed (in this case, goods or services), but about the underlying emotions and psychological patterns that drive it.

At its core, shopping addiction is about the temporary relief that buying something provides. For many, it offers a momentary escape from negative emotions such as anxiety, sadness, or boredom. The act of purchasing triggers a short-term feeling of satisfaction or excitement, almost like a "high." However, once that feeling fades, the guilt, regret, or financial stress takes its place, leading the person to shop again in search of that fleeting sense of relief. This vicious cycle of buy-regret-buy can spiral out of control, often leaving individuals with mounting debt, strained relationships, and deeper emotional struggles.

How Common is 'Shopping Addiction'

In the U.S. there is a **5.8%** prevalence of occuring

- A person is obsessed with the action of shopping
- There is some level of pre-purchase anxiety and a strong need to shop
- Shopping makes them feel good

Prevalence of Shopping Addiction. Source: fherehab.com

While shopping addiction can affect anyone, it is often linked to certain emotional or psychological factors. For some, shopping becomes a way to fill emotional voids or cope with unresolved issues. For others, it may serve as a way to boost self-esteem or project a certain image to the world. Many people with shopping addiction also struggle with other mental health issues, such as anxiety, depression, or impulse control disorders, which can make breaking the cycle even more challenging.

What makes shopping addiction particularly difficult to recognize and address is that it's not just about excessive spending. A person with this addiction may buy things they don't need, but it's the compulsive nature of the behavior—the inability to stop even when they know it's harmful—that signals a deeper issue. Shopping becomes less about the actual purchase and more about the emotional relief it promises, even if that relief is temporary.

This form of addiction is often overlooked because it doesn't always carry the same visible consequences as other addictions like alcohol or drugs. Yet the impact can be just as destructive. Financial difficulties are often the most visible sign, but the emotional toll can be significant, affecting self-esteem, relationships, and overall well-being. People struggling with shopping addiction may hide purchases, feel ashamed, or lie about their spending habits, which only deepens their feelings of isolation and guilt.

Understanding what shopping addiction truly is and recognizing the signs can be the first step toward breaking free from its hold. It's important to see it not as a lack of willpower or self-control, but as a real psychological issue that requires understanding, support, and practical solutions.

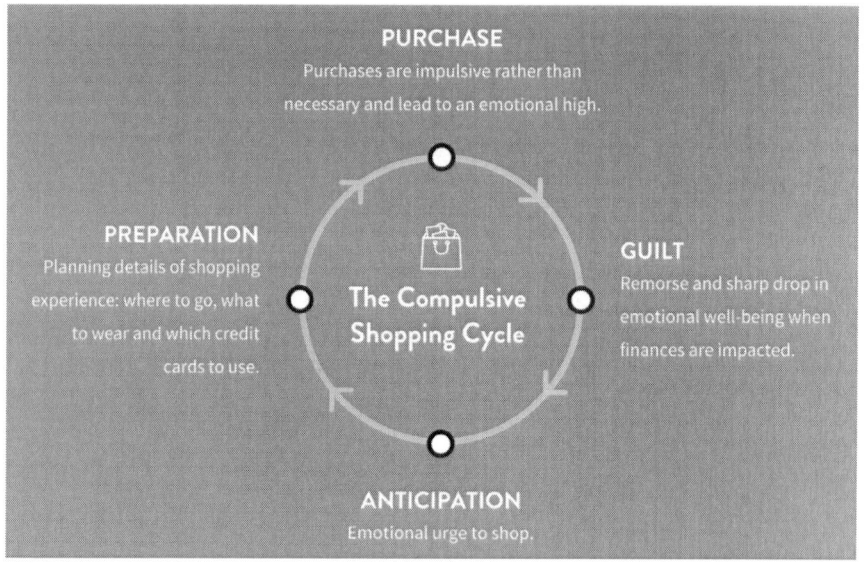

The Compulsive Shopping Cycle. Source: moneygeek.com

Signs of Shopping Addiction

Shopping addiction can often be difficult to recognize, especially in a world where spending is encouraged and even celebrated. However, the signs of compulsive buying go beyond enjoying a shopping spree or treating yourself now and then. It's about shopping that begins to feel out of control, where the consequences are no longer worth the thrill of the purchase. Let's look at some key signs that may indicate shopping has turned from a healthy habit into a harmful addiction.

One of the most common signs of shopping addiction is frequent impulse buying. You may find yourself purchasing items you didn't plan to buy, often without considering whether you truly need them. This can happen both in physical stores and online, and it's often driven by a sudden desire to own something, rather than by a practical need.

Another indicator is the feeling of euphoria or excitement during the shopping process, often followed by guilt or regret. Many people with shopping addiction experience a rush of excitement when they're making a purchase, only to feel a deep sense of regret once the item is bought. This emotional rollercoaster is a hallmark of addiction because it reveals how shopping serves as a temporary escape or emotional high.

You may also notice difficulty controlling the urge to shop, even when you know it's causing harm. People struggling with this addiction often make promises to themselves to stop shopping or cut back, only to break those promises soon after. There's a constant internal battle between the desire to stop and the overwhelming urge to continue.

Financial problems are another clear sign. Racking up debt, emptying savings, or constantly living paycheck to paycheck due to shopping habits are major red flags. If you find yourself hiding purchases, credit card bills, or bank statements from family and friends, it's likely that your shopping has crossed the line from occasional indulgence to a serious problem.

Shopping addiction doesn't only affect your bank account; it also impacts your emotional well-being. Feelings of anxiety, stress, or depression often accompany the addiction, especially when you can't afford to shop or are trying to reduce your spending. Over time, compulsive buying can create a vicious cycle where shopping is used to cope with negative emotions, only to worsen those feelings in the long run.

If shopping begins to interfere with your relationships, that's another warning sign. You may lie about your purchases, argue with loved ones over your spending habits, or withdraw from social situations to shop in secret. The isolation and secrecy surrounding shopping addiction can strain even the closest relationships.

Recognizing these signs is the first step toward change. It's easy to dismiss overspending as a harmless habit, but when shopping starts to control your life, finances, and emotions, it's time to take a closer look at what's really going on.

Awareness opens the door to understanding, and from there, real progress can begin.

The Science Behind It

Shopping addiction, like many other compulsive behaviors, is deeply rooted in how our brains process rewards. When we shop, especially when we purchase something new or exciting, our brain releases a chemical called dopamine. Dopamine is often referred to as the "feel-good" neurotransmitter because it plays a key role in the pleasure and reward systems of the brain. This surge of dopamine creates a sense of excitement or happiness, which explains the temporary "high" people feel after making a purchase.

However, this rush of dopamine doesn't last long. Once the initial excitement wears off, many people are left with feelings of guilt or regret, especially if the purchase was unnecessary or impulsive. Despite these negative feelings, the brain still craves that dopamine boost, leading to a cycle of repeated shopping to chase the same high. This pattern mirrors the way other addictions work, such as gambling or substance abuse, where the pursuit of short-term pleasure leads to long-term consequences.

Another factor that influences shopping addiction is the way our brains process instant gratification. In a world where shopping is easier than ever—thanks to online stores and one-click purchases—our ability to delay gratification becomes weaker. The more we give in to the temptation of buying something right away, the more our brain associates shopping with instant pleasure. This makes it harder to resist future impulses.

On top of that, there is the psychological phenomenon known as "buyer's remorse." This occurs when the emotional rush of making a purchase fades, and reality sets in. People begin to question whether they needed the item, if they spent too much, or if they acted out of emotion rather than logic. While these feelings might deter some people from future purchases, others might feel overwhelmed by guilt and shame, which can drive them to shop again as a way of coping with those negative emotions.

Additionally, our brains are wired to respond to scarcity and limited-time offers. Marketing tactics like flash sales, countdown timers, and "only a few left" messages exploit our natural fear of missing out. This triggers an emotional response that pushes us to act quickly, bypassing our usual decision-making process. Our brains perceive the potential loss of an opportunity as more significant than the actual benefit of the purchase itself.

In essence, shopping addiction isn't just about the act of buying. It's about the powerful chemical reactions in our brains that influence behavior, emotions, and decision-making. Understanding the science behind it can help us recognize why breaking free from shopping addiction is not simply a matter of willpower—it's about retraining the brain and finding healthier ways to seek pleasure and manage stress.

Chapter 2

Why Do We Shop?

Emotional Triggers and Shopping

At the heart of many shopping addictions lies a powerful force: emotion. Shopping often becomes more than just a way to buy things we need; it becomes an outlet for handling the emotions we struggle with. The link between emotions and spending is strong, and for many people, shopping offers a brief moment of relief from deeper feelings they may not want to face.

One of the most common emotional triggers for shopping is stress. Whether it's work deadlines, financial pressures, or personal conflicts, stress can build up and leave us looking for ways to cope. Shopping offers a quick distraction and can make us feel momentarily in control of our lives, even if the relief is only temporary. The act of buying something new creates a sense of achievement or reward, even though the underlying stress remains untouched.

Loneliness is another key trigger. When people feel disconnected or isolated, shopping can fill that emotional gap by providing a momentary sense of connection or fulfillment. The excitement of receiving a new purchase, whether it's delivered to your door or picked up in a store, can serve as a distraction from feelings of isolation. However, this satisfaction is often short-lived, and the loneliness returns, leading to more shopping in an attempt to fill the void.

Boredom can also push people toward shopping as a way to break the monotony. When life feels dull or repetitive, the stimulation of browsing stores or scrolling through shopping apps offers a spark of excitement. It gives the brain something new to focus on and provides an easy way to pass the time. Over time, this behavior can become habitual, with shopping becoming the go-to solution for any idle moment.

Another significant emotional driver is low self-esteem. People who struggle with their self-worth may shop in an attempt to feel better about themselves. Purchasing new clothes, accessories, or even luxury items can create the illusion of confidence or success. The idea of looking better or owning the latest trendy item can give a temporary boost to one's self-image. Unfortunately, these feelings often fade, leaving the shopper to face their insecurities again.

Sadness or depression can lead to what is often called "retail therapy." In these moments, shopping feels like a way to self-soothe, lifting the spirits through the temporary excitement of buying something new. However, the underlying sadness or depression doesn't go away, and in many cases, the act of overspending can worsen those feelings, especially if financial stress adds to the emotional burden.

Understanding the connection between emotions and shopping is crucial for anyone trying to break free from compulsive buying. When we start to recognize how our feelings drive our spending, we can begin to develop healthier ways of coping with stress, loneliness, boredom, or low self-esteem. Instead of turning to shopping for comfort, finding alternative outlets, such as talking to a friend, engaging in a hobby, or practicing mindfulness, can offer more lasting emotional relief.

Shopping might feel like a quick fix, but its effects are temporary. Recognizing emotional triggers and understanding how they fuel shopping behavior is the first step in breaking the cycle and taking control of both your emotions and your spending.

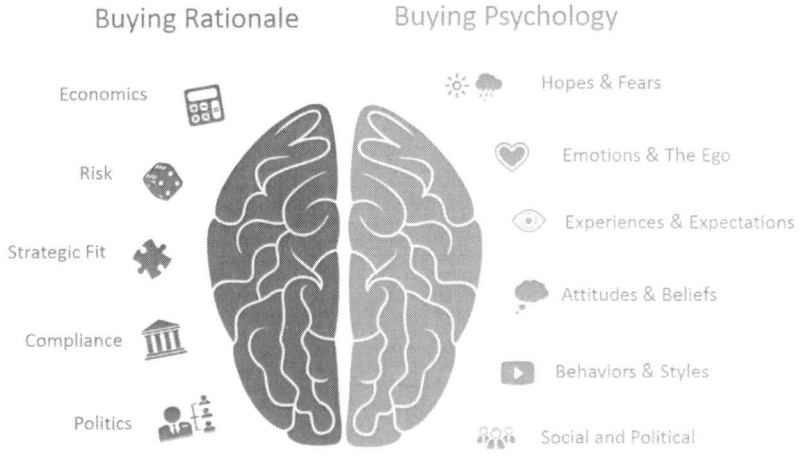

Psychological Purchasing Triggers. Source: zeve.au

The Influence of Consumer Culture

In today's world, we are constantly surrounded by messages encouraging us to buy more. From flashy advertisements on social media to endless sales in stores, consumer culture has become a powerful force shaping how we live and how we spend. Shopping is no longer just about fulfilling needs; it's become a way to express ourselves, keep up with trends, and even find comfort during tough times.

One of the driving factors behind consumer culture is advertising. Everywhere we look, we are exposed to ads that tell us we need the latest phone, the newest fashion, or the most advanced gadget. These messages often appeal to our emotions, suggesting that buying a particular product will make us happier, more attractive, or more successful. Over time, this constant bombardment of marketing makes it difficult to separate what we truly need from what we're told we should want.

Social media has amplified this even further. Platforms like Instagram, TikTok, and Facebook have turned into virtual marketplaces where influencers promote products, and advertisements are seamlessly woven into our feeds. The rise of "influencer culture" means that people we follow and admire are often subtly (or not so subtly) selling us products. Whether it's a beauty product, a designer handbag, or the latest tech accessory, social media has made shopping feel like an essential part of belonging and fitting in.

The convenience of online shopping has also played a big role in the rise of consumer culture. With just a few clicks, you can have almost anything delivered to your doorstep. Retailers have made it incredibly easy to shop anytime, anywhere, and this instant gratification can be hard to resist. Whether it's a midnight purchase or a quick scroll during a lunch break, the ease of online shopping has blurred the lines between want and need.

Sales tactics like "limited-time offers" and "exclusive deals" also feed into this culture, making us feel like we're missing out if we don't act fast. Retailers often create a sense of urgency that pressures us to buy now, even if we don't really need the item. This fear of missing out, or FOMO, taps into a deeper desire to not fall behind or miss opportunities, driving more impulsive shopping.

At the heart of consumer culture is the belief that buying more will bring happiness. We are constantly told that material possessions will improve our lives, whether by boosting our self-esteem, making us more popular, or solving our problems. This message is reinforced through ads, movies, TV shows, and even the people around us. As a result, shopping becomes not just an activity, but a way of coping with emotions, achieving status, and shaping our identities.

However, this cycle of consumption can lead to a sense of emptiness. The excitement of a new purchase is often short-lived, leaving us craving more. As we accumulate more things, we can start to feel overwhelmed by clutter, debt, and dissatisfaction. Consumer culture pushes us to believe that the next purchase will be the one that finally brings lasting happiness, but that fulfillment often remains out of reach.

Understanding how consumer culture influences our shopping habits is a key step toward breaking free from the constant pressure to buy. It allows us to pause and reflect on why we're making certain purchases, helping us make more intentional and mindful decisions.

The Retail Therapy Myth

For many people, the idea of "retail therapy" seems harmless. After all, what could be wrong with treating yourself to something nice after a tough day? The concept of retail therapy has been embraced in popular culture as a quick fix for dealing with stress, sadness, or boredom. The thought of buying something to feel better can be tempting, and in the moment, it often works. But the relief that comes from shopping is short-lived, and the emotional issues remain beneath the surface.

Retail therapy gives the illusion that buying things will bring comfort or happiness, but the truth is that this kind of shopping rarely addresses the deeper emotional needs driving the behavior. Shopping can provide a temporary distraction or a quick boost of excitement, but it doesn't resolve the feelings that led you to shop in the first place. In fact, it can often make things worse, leaving you with more financial stress or a lingering sense of guilt once the high fades.

One of the reasons why retail therapy feels so appealing is the way it taps into the brain's reward system. When you make a purchase, your brain releases dopamine, the chemical responsible for pleasure and reward. This creates a sense of satisfaction or happiness, even if the purchase was unnecessary or impulsive. However, this rush fades quickly, and you may find yourself needing to shop again to recapture that same feeling. This can create a cycle where shopping becomes a go-to coping mechanism, even though it never truly addresses the underlying emotions.

Another problem with the retail therapy myth is that it can mask more serious emotional or mental health issues. Feelings of sadness, loneliness, anxiety, or boredom are often at the root of compulsive shopping, but retail therapy does little to alleviate these emotions. In fact, relying on shopping as a form of emotional escape can make it harder to recognize and deal with these feelings in healthy ways. Over time, it becomes easier to reach for your credit card than to confront the real issues that need attention.

The financial consequences of retail therapy can't be ignored, either. While a small purchase here and there might seem harmless, frequent reliance on shopping to lift your mood can lead to mounting debt and financial strain. The temporary relief you feel in the moment can quickly turn into regret when the bills start piling up. This can create a vicious cycle, where shopping causes financial stress, which in turn leads to more emotional distress, prompting even more shopping in an attempt to feel better.

Retail therapy may offer a momentary break from your worries, but it's important to recognize it for what it is: a short-term distraction that doesn't solve the real problem. True emotional healing comes from finding healthier ways to manage your feelings, whether that's through talking to someone you trust, engaging in activities that bring you joy, or seeking professional help when needed. Shopping can never fill the emotional voids you may be trying to escape. Recognizing this is the first step toward breaking free from the retail therapy myth and building healthier habits that lead to lasting fulfillment.

Chapter 3

Breaking the Cycle

Recognizing Your Triggers

One of the most important steps in overcoming shopping addiction is understanding what drives the impulse to shop. These triggers can be emotional, environmental, or even social, and recognizing them is key to breaking the cycle of compulsive spending. Once you become aware of the situations or feelings that lead you to shop, you can begin to address the root causes of your behavior and develop healthier coping strategies.

For many people, emotional triggers play a major role in their shopping habits. Emotions such as stress, sadness, boredom, or even loneliness can push someone to seek comfort or distraction through shopping. The act of buying something new can temporarily lift your mood or provide a sense of control in a moment of emotional turmoil. However, this relief is often short-lived, and the underlying emotions remain, leaving you with the same feelings and potentially new financial worries.

Stress is one of the most common triggers. When life becomes overwhelming, whether due to work, relationships, or personal challenges, shopping may feel like a quick way to escape or reward yourself. A difficult day at the office can end with an online shopping spree, or a personal setback might lead to an impulse purchase to fill the emotional gap. The key is to recognize that these moments of stress are fueling your urge to shop and to find alternative ways to manage that stress without resorting to spending.

Boredom can also be a powerful trigger for shopping. In today's digital world, it's incredibly easy to fill idle time by browsing online stores. With so many options available at your fingertips, shopping becomes an activity that not only fills time but also provides an instant dopamine boost. Recognizing boredom as a trigger can help you shift your focus to more productive activities that don't involve shopping, such as reading, exercising, or pursuing a hobby.

Social triggers are another factor to be aware of. Social media platforms are filled with influencers and advertisements that encourage us to buy the latest products, creating a sense of pressure to keep up with trends. Friends and family may also contribute, whether through their own spending habits or through group activities that involve shopping. You may feel the need to shop to fit in or to avoid missing out, even if you don't truly want or need the items you're purchasing.

Environmental triggers can also play a significant role. Walking through a mall or receiving constant promotional emails can spark the desire to shop, even if you weren't planning to. Online shopping platforms use tactics like personalized recommendations and special discounts to draw you in, making it harder to resist the temptation to buy. By identifying the specific environments or situations that lead to impulse shopping, you can take steps to limit your exposure and create boundaries that support your recovery.

Recognizing your personal triggers is about becoming more mindful of the moments that lead you to shop. Once you are aware of these triggers, you can start developing healthier coping mechanisms and making more intentional choices when the urge to shop arises. This awareness is the first step toward regaining control over your spending habits and breaking free from the cycle of addiction.

Mindfulness and Emotional Regulation

When it comes to managing shopping addiction, understanding your emotions is crucial. Many people turn to shopping as a way to cope with stress, anxiety, or boredom without fully realizing what they are feeling or why. This is where mindfulness comes in. Mindfulness helps you become more aware of your thoughts, emotions, and behaviors in the present moment, allowing you to understand your triggers and respond to them in healthier ways.

Mindfulness involves paying attention to what you're feeling without judgment. It's about noticing when you're drawn to shop and asking yourself, "What am I really feeling right now?" Are you stressed after a long day, feeling lonely, or simply bored? Becoming aware of these emotions is the first step in learning how to manage them without turning to shopping for relief.

One of the key benefits of mindfulness is that it helps you create space between your emotions and your actions. Instead of immediately reacting to an emotional trigger with a shopping spree, mindfulness gives you a moment to pause and reflect. In that pause, you can make a conscious choice to do something different—whether it's taking a walk, talking to a friend, or practicing a relaxation technique. Over time, this practice strengthens your ability to regulate your emotions without relying on shopping as a crutch.

Emotional regulation is the ability to manage your emotional responses in a healthy and balanced way. It's not about suppressing or ignoring your feelings, but about learning how to handle them in a way that doesn't lead to impulsive behavior like overspending. By practicing emotional regulation, you develop the skills to recognize what you're feeling and respond to it in a way that aligns with your long-term goals, like saving money or reducing debt.

For example, if you notice that you tend to shop when you're feeling anxious, mindfulness can help you identify that pattern. From there, emotional regulation techniques—such as deep breathing, meditation, or simply taking a break—can help you manage that anxiety without turning to shopping for relief. The more you practice these techniques, the easier it becomes to handle your emotions without impulsive spending.

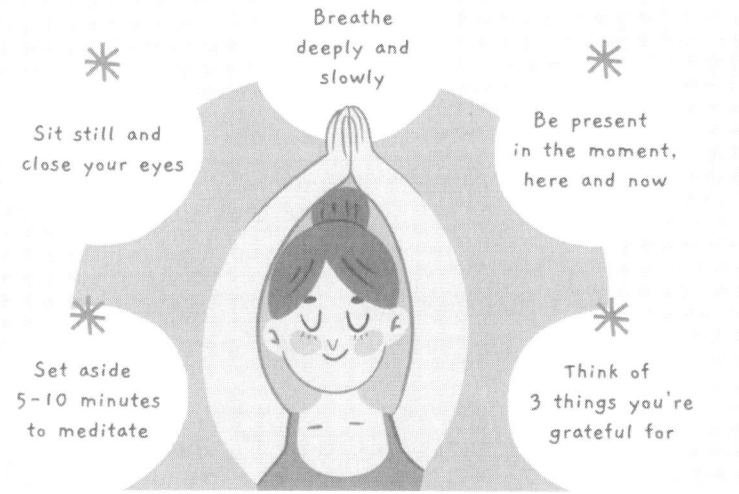

Mindfulness Techniques for Emotional Regulation. Source: linkedin.com

Mindfulness and emotional regulation work hand-in-hand to help you break the cycle of shopping addiction. By staying present and aware of your emotions, and learning how to manage them effectively, you can begin to shift your relationship with shopping. Instead of using it as a way to escape or soothe uncomfortable feelings, you can find healthier ways to cope and, in the process, regain control over both your emotions and your spending habits.

Building Self-Awareness

Developing self-awareness is a crucial step in breaking free from shopping addiction. Self-awareness involves understanding your thoughts, emotions, and behaviors, and how they influence your decisions. When you are aware of what drives you to shop, you gain the power to make more intentional and informed choices, rather than simply reacting to impulses.

One of the first steps in building self-awareness is paying attention to the thoughts and feelings you experience before, during, and after shopping. Ask yourself, "What am I feeling right now?" or "Why do I want to buy this item?" This simple act of pausing and reflecting can reveal a lot about your motivations. You might discover that you're feeling stressed, anxious, or lonely, and that shopping is an attempt to manage those emotions. Recognizing this pattern is the first step toward finding healthier ways to cope.

Self-awareness also means being honest with yourself about your needs versus your wants. It's easy to convince yourself that a purchase is necessary when, in reality, it's driven by desire or impulse. Start by questioning whether the items you buy are truly essential, or if they serve to fill an emotional void. This level of honesty requires practice, but over time, it helps you make decisions that align with your long-term goals, rather than giving in to short-term satisfaction.

A helpful technique in building self-awareness is keeping a journal of your spending habits. Writing down what you purchase, along with the reasons behind those purchases, can shed light on patterns you may not have noticed before. Are you more likely to shop after a tough day at work? Do certain environments or people make you more likely to spend? By tracking these moments, you start to connect the dots between your emotions, triggers, and spending habits.

Another key aspect of self-awareness is understanding how shopping fits into your identity. For many people, shopping is tied to how they see themselves or how they want others to perceive them. You may use shopping to project a certain image, boost your self-esteem, or gain a sense of control. Becoming aware of these deeper motivations can help you separate your sense of self from your possessions, and realize that your worth isn't determined by what you own.

Building self-awareness is not about judgment or self-criticism. It's about observing your behavior with curiosity and compassion, allowing yourself to understand why you make the choices you do. With this understanding, you can begin to shift your mindset and behaviors in ways that serve your overall well-being, rather than feeding into an addictive cycle.

The more you practice self-awareness, the more empowered you become to make conscious, thoughtful decisions about your spending. Over time, you'll find that being in tune with your emotions and motivations helps you break the cycle of compulsive shopping and develop healthier, more sustainable habits.

Chapter 4

Reclaiming Financial Control

Assessing the Damage

When you realize that shopping has become more than just an occasional indulgence, it's important to take a step back and assess the impact it has had on your life. This isn't always easy, as the consequences of compulsive shopping can build up gradually over time. However, understanding the full scope of the damage is essential for moving forward and regaining control over your spending habits.

Start with your financial situation. One of the most obvious effects of shopping addiction is the strain it places on your finances. Take an honest look at your bank accounts, credit card balances, and any outstanding loans. How much debt have you accumulated? Are you able to make your payments on time, or are you struggling to keep up? Looking at the numbers may feel uncomfortable, but it's a necessary part of understanding how shopping has affected your financial health. Once you know where you stand, you can begin to plan how to repair the damage.

Next, consider the emotional toll. Shopping addiction often leaves behind more than just financial consequences; it can also take a serious emotional toll. Feelings of guilt, shame, and anxiety frequently accompany compulsive buying. You may have experienced regret after making purchases or felt overwhelmed by the constant pressure to spend. Reflecting on these emotional impacts helps you understand how deeply the addiction has affected your well-being, beyond just the financial strain.

Shopping addiction can also harm your relationships. You may have found yourself hiding purchases from loved ones or lying about your spending. Financial problems caused by overspending can lead to arguments and increased stress within relationships. If you've noticed tension or conflict in your personal life as a result of your shopping habits, it's important to recognize this as part of the broader impact of the addiction. Taking responsibility for how your actions have affected those around you is a key step toward rebuilding trust and repairing these relationships.

Finally, assess how shopping has influenced your quality of life. Has overspending prevented you from reaching important financial goals, like saving for a house or retirement? Have you had to give up other activities or experiences because of financial constraints caused by shopping? Compulsive buying often limits your freedom and ability to live the life you truly want, as money is continually drained by unnecessary purchases. Identifying these sacrifices can motivate you to make lasting changes.

Assessing the damage isn't about punishing yourself for past mistakes. It's about gaining clarity on where you are and what needs to be done to move forward. Once you have a clear picture of the financial, emotional, and relational consequences of shopping addiction, you can begin taking steps to address them, empowering yourself to make positive changes for the future.

Creating a Realistic Budget

Building a realistic budget is a vital step in managing your finances and breaking free from shopping addiction. A budget gives you control over your money, helps you track where it's going, and ensures that your spending aligns with your priorities and goals. The key to making a budget that works is keeping it simple, flexible, and grounded in your actual needs and financial situation.

The first step in creating a budget is understanding your current financial picture. Begin by taking a close look at your income. This includes not only your salary but also any other sources of income, such as freelance work, investments, or side jobs. Knowing exactly how much money you have coming in each month sets the foundation for planning where your money should go.

Next, it's important to assess your expenses. Start by listing all your fixed expenses—those that remain the same every month—such as rent or mortgage payments, utilities, insurance, and debt repayments. Then, move on to your variable expenses, which can fluctuate, like groceries, transportation, and entertainment. Be honest with yourself about your spending habits, including the small, often-overlooked expenses that can add up, like coffee runs or impulse buys.

One of the most helpful aspects of a budget is giving yourself a clear limit for discretionary spending. This is where many people get off track, as discretionary purchases are often linked to emotional triggers or habits. By setting a realistic spending limit in this category, you can still enjoy occasional treats or outings without feeling deprived, while also ensuring that you don't overspend.

A good budget also includes room for savings. It's important to prioritize setting aside a portion of your income each month, even if it's a small amount. Your savings can act as a financial cushion for emergencies, but it can also help you work toward long-term goals, such as buying a home or taking a vacation. Having these goals in mind makes it easier to resist the urge to splurge on unnecessary purchases.

Flexibility is crucial when creating a budget that you can stick to. Life is unpredictable, and sometimes unexpected expenses arise. Your budget shouldn't feel like a rigid rulebook, but rather a guide that helps you make smart choices. If one month brings an unforeseen cost, you can adjust other areas of your budget to accommodate it. The goal is not perfection but consistency and awareness.

Lastly, it's important to regularly review your budget. At the end of each month, take a moment to assess how well you stuck to your plan. If you went over in certain areas, don't beat yourself up—use it as a learning opportunity to adjust your spending or refine your budget for the next month. Over time, as you get more comfortable with budgeting, you'll find that it becomes easier to manage your money, reduce financial stress, and avoid compulsive shopping.

Creating a realistic budget isn't just about limiting spending. It's about giving yourself control and clarity over your financial life. A well-planned budget helps you align your money with your values and goals, empowering you to make decisions that support your long-term well-being.

Housing
25-30%
Mortgage, rent, HOA fees, taxes, etc.

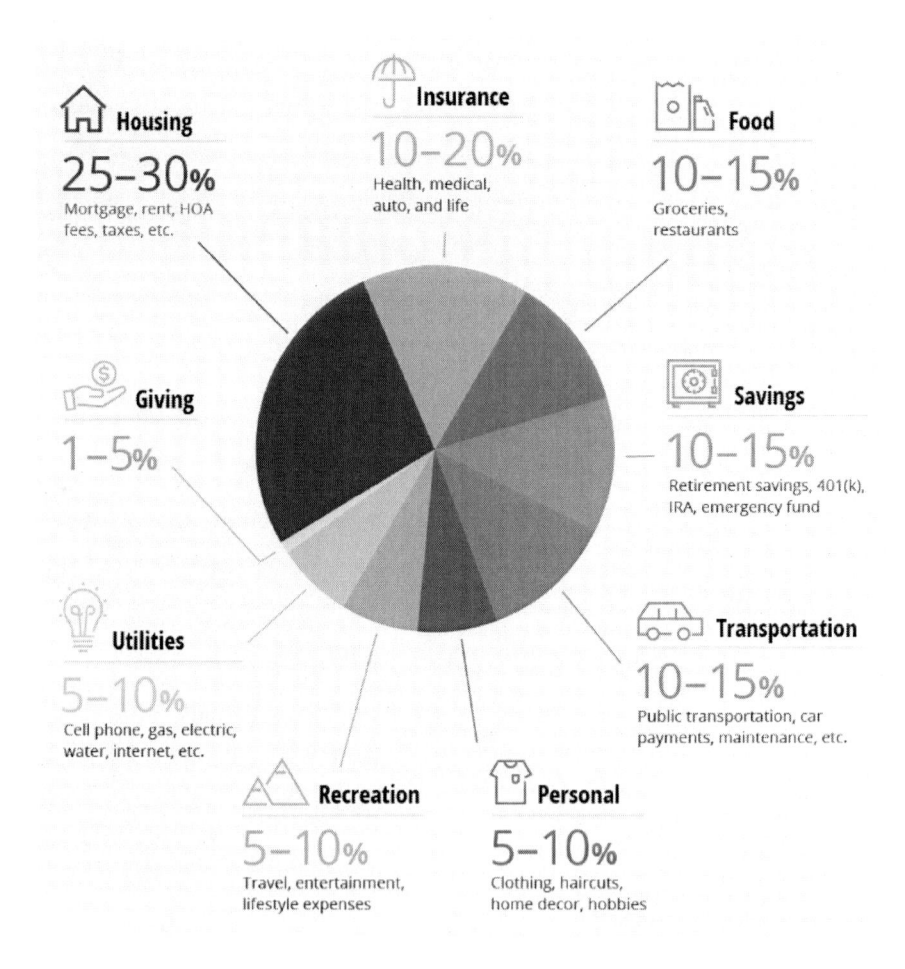

Insurance
10-20%
Health, medical, auto, and life

Food
10-15%
Groceries, restaurants

Giving
1-5%

Savings
10-15%
Retirement savings, 401(k), IRA, emergency fund

Utilities
5-10%
Cell phone, gas, electric, water, internet, etc.

Transportation
10-15%
Public transportation, car payments, maintenance, etc.

Recreation
5-10%
Travel, entertainment, lifestyle expenses

Personal
5-10%
Clothing, haircuts, home decor, hobbies

Budget Allocation Breakdown. Source: fultonbank.com

Debt Recovery Strategies

Facing debt can feel overwhelming, especially when it's the result of shopping addiction. However, recovering from debt is not impossible, and with the right strategies, you can begin to regain control of your finances and work your way toward a more secure financial future. It's important to remember that this process takes time, but every step you take brings you closer to financial freedom.

The first strategy for recovering from debt is to get organized. Start by gathering all of your financial information. This includes credit card statements, loan balances, and any other outstanding debts. Make a list of each debt, noting the total amount owed, the interest rate, and the minimum monthly payment. By getting a clear picture of what you owe, you'll be able to create a plan that's realistic and manageable.

Next, focus on budgeting. A solid budget is essential to managing debt effectively. Track your income and expenses carefully to see where your money is going each month. This will help you identify areas where you can cut back and free up extra funds to put toward your debt payments. Remember that the goal of budgeting isn't to restrict yourself completely but to find a balance that allows you to pay off your debts while still meeting your essential needs.

One popular debt repayment method is the debt snowball approach. This strategy involves focusing on paying off your smallest debts first while continuing to make minimum payments on the rest. Once the smallest debt is fully paid off, you move on to the next smallest debt, using the money you were paying toward the first debt to accelerate the payments. This method gives you quick wins, which can build motivation as you eliminate smaller balances.

Another option is the debt avalanche method, which focuses on paying off debts with the highest interest rates first. This approach can save you more money in the long run, as it reduces the amount of interest you'll pay overall. Both the debt snowball and debt avalanche methods can be effective, so choose the one that feels right for your situation.

If your debts feel overwhelming, consider negotiating with creditors. Many creditors are willing to work with you if you reach out and explain your situation. You may be able to negotiate lower interest rates, reduced payments, or even settle a debt for less than the full amount owed. Be honest and proactive in your communication with creditors, as this can often lead to more favorable repayment terms.

For those struggling to manage debt on their own, seeking professional help can be a game-changer. Financial advisors or credit counseling services can provide expert guidance and help you create a tailored debt repayment plan. They may also be able to help you consolidate your debts, which involves combining multiple debts into a single loan with a lower interest rate. Debt consolidation can make your payments more manageable and reduce the total amount of interest you'll pay over time.

Finally, it's important to stay committed to your debt recovery plan. There may be setbacks along the way, but persistence is key. Celebrate small victories as you pay off each debt, and keep your long-term financial goals in mind. Over time, you'll begin to see progress, and with each step forward, you'll feel more in control of your finances.

Debt recovery is not an overnight process, but with organization, a solid budget, and the right repayment strategy, you can take meaningful steps toward a debt-free future. Every payment you make is a step closer to financial freedom, and with perseverance, you'll get there.

Chapter 5

Practical Strategies to Stop Shopping

How to Control Shopping Impulses

Controlling shopping impulses is a challenge, especially in a world where buying is as easy as a click or a quick swipe. However, with the right strategies, it's entirely possible to manage those urges and make more thoughtful decisions about your purchases. The key is to slow down the process, create space between the impulse and the action, and find alternative ways to meet the emotional needs driving the desire to shop.

One of the most effective ways to control shopping impulses is to introduce a pause before making any purchase. Whenever you feel the urge to buy something, give yourself a set waiting period—whether it's 24 hours, a week, or even longer. This time allows you to step back from the emotional high of the moment and reconsider whether the item is something you truly need or just something you want in the moment. More often than not, the impulse will fade, and you'll realize that the purchase wasn't necessary.

Another helpful approach is to remove temptation from your environment. If online shopping is a major source of your spending, consider unsubscribing from promotional emails or removing shopping apps from your phone. Out of sight often means out of mind. Similarly, avoiding frequent trips to malls or stores can reduce the temptation to buy things on a whim. You might even consider creating a block on certain websites during your most vulnerable times, such as late at night or after a stressful day.

Mindfulness is another powerful tool in controlling shopping impulses. Being mindful means being fully aware of your thoughts, feelings, and actions in the present moment. When you notice the urge to shop, pause and check in with yourself. Ask, "What am I feeling right now? Am I bored, stressed, or anxious?" By identifying the emotion behind the impulse, you can work on addressing that feeling in healthier ways, such as taking a walk, talking to a friend, or practicing relaxation techniques.

It's also important to identify patterns in your shopping behavior. For example, do you tend to shop when you're feeling lonely? Is it a way to reward yourself after a tough week? Understanding the underlying emotional triggers that lead to shopping can help you create strategies to cope with those feelings without turning to spending. Keeping a journal where you track your mood and spending habits can provide valuable insights into your patterns.

One strategy that can help reduce impulsive shopping is setting clear financial goals. When you have specific goals in mind, such as saving for a vacation, paying off debt, or building an emergency fund, it becomes easier to resist impulsive purchases. Every time you feel the urge to shop, remind yourself of these goals and consider how the purchase might delay your progress. This shift in perspective can help you stay focused on your long-term financial well-being rather than short-term gratification.

Lastly, you can also try implementing a reward system for yourself, but one that doesn't involve shopping. For instance, treat yourself to a favorite activity or spend time doing something you enjoy, like reading, exercising, or exploring a new hobby. These non-material rewards can offer the same sense of satisfaction and fulfillment without the need for spending.

Controlling shopping impulses is about building awareness, patience, and finding healthier ways to meet your emotional needs. With time and practice, you'll develop greater control over your spending and feel more empowered in your relationship with money.

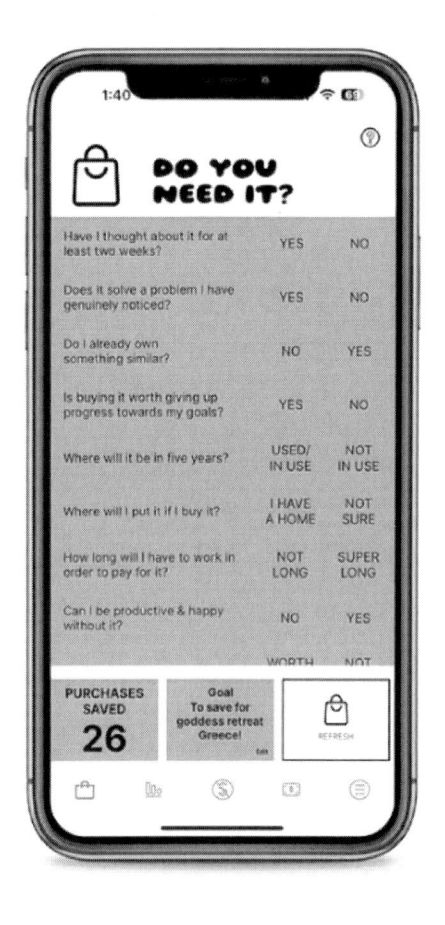

(Stop Impulse Buying) App Interface. Source: stopimpulse.com

Establishing New Habits

Breaking free from shopping addiction requires more than just stopping harmful behaviors—it's about replacing them with new, healthier habits that support your long-term goals. Establishing new habits can be challenging, but it is one of the most powerful tools you have to regain control over your spending and build a more balanced life. The key is to focus on small, consistent changes that, over time, create lasting improvements.

The first step in creating new habits is recognizing your triggers. These are the situations, emotions, or thoughts that lead you to shop impulsively. Once you're aware of what prompts your shopping urges, you can begin to plan alternative actions. For example, if stress drives you to shop, consider healthier outlets for managing stress, like exercising, meditating, or journaling. The goal is to find new activities that fulfill the emotional needs previously met by shopping.

One habit that can help you break the cycle of overspending is pausing before making a purchase. Instead of buying something on impulse, practice waiting at least 24 hours before making a decision. This gives you time to consider whether the purchase is truly necessary or if it's just a response to an emotional trigger. Often, after waiting, the urge to buy will fade, and you'll realize the purchase wasn't as important as it initially seemed.

Another important habit is setting specific financial goals. Whether it's saving for a vacation, building an emergency fund, or paying off debt, having clear goals gives you a reason to say no to unnecessary spending. When you're tempted to buy something, remind yourself of your larger financial priorities and how each small decision can bring you closer to achieving them.

Developing a healthy reward system can also help. Many people turn to shopping as a way to reward themselves, but there are plenty of other ways to celebrate achievements or lift your mood. Consider non-monetary rewards like spending time with loved ones, enjoying a favorite hobby, or treating yourself to a relaxing day. By shifting the focus away from material items, you can start to associate happiness and fulfillment with experiences rather than possessions.

Creating a budget is another habit that will serve you well on your journey to financial control. When you know exactly where your money is going and how much you have available to spend, you're less likely to make impulsive purchases. A budget helps you stay accountable to yourself and ensures that your spending aligns with your long-term goals.

Building these new habits takes time and patience, but consistency is the key to success. Each day, focus on making one small change, whether that's pausing before a purchase, reviewing your budget, or engaging in a new hobby. Over time, these small changes will compound, and you'll begin to notice a shift in your relationship with shopping. What once felt like an uncontrollable urge will gradually be replaced by more thoughtful, intentional choices that support a healthier and more balanced lifestyle.

Managing Online Shopping

In today's world, online shopping is more accessible than ever before. With a few clicks or taps, you can have almost anything delivered to your doorstep. While this convenience has its advantages, it also makes it easy to lose track of spending and fall into the habit of impulsive buying. Managing online shopping effectively is about regaining control, setting boundaries, and becoming more intentional with your purchases.

One of the first steps to managing online shopping is to limit your exposure to the constant barrage of deals and advertisements. Online retailers are experts at drawing you in with flash sales, discounts, and personalized recommendations. Unsubscribing from promotional emails, disabling notifications from shopping apps, and using ad blockers can significantly reduce the temptation to buy things you don't really need. The less you're exposed to these prompts, the easier it is to stay focused on what truly matters.

Another helpful tactic is to avoid saving your payment information on websites. While having your credit card details pre-filled at checkout might save time, it also makes it too easy to make quick, impulsive purchases. By removing your payment information, you introduce a pause in the process, giving yourself more time to reconsider whether the purchase is necessary. The extra step of entering your card details manually can provide just enough of a barrier to help you rethink the decision.

Creating a budget specifically for online shopping is another effective way to stay in control. Set aside a certain amount each month that you can spend on online purchases, and stick to it. Knowing that you have a limit helps you make more thoughtful decisions, as you'll need to prioritize what you really want or need. Tracking your online spending regularly can also give you a clearer picture of where your money is going and help you avoid surprises at the end of the month.

Wishlist tools offered by many online retailers can also be valuable for managing impulses. Instead of buying something immediately, add it to your wishlist and wait a few days before making a decision. This delay gives you time to reflect on whether the item is truly necessary or just an emotional response in the moment. More often than not, the urge to buy fades, and you may find that you no longer want the item.

If online shopping has become a way to fill emotional voids, it's important to find alternatives to meet those needs. Shopping can often be a way to distract from boredom, loneliness, or stress, but these feelings can be addressed in healthier ways. Engaging in activities that bring you joy, such as hobbies, exercise, or connecting with others, can provide the fulfillment you're seeking without the need to spend money.

Lastly, consider using apps or browser extensions that help you manage your online shopping habits. Some tools track price changes, so you can avoid buying something impulsively and wait for the best deal. Others can block shopping sites during certain hours or set spending limits for specific categories. These digital tools can act as helpful guards, keeping you accountable and preventing overspending.

Managing online shopping is about becoming more mindful of your habits and making intentional choices. With a few adjustments, you can still enjoy the convenience of shopping online without letting it take control of your finances or emotional well-being.

How Well Do You Manage Your Shopping Habits?

Purpose of the Quiz:

This quiz helps you assess your relationship with shopping, identify strengths and areas for improvement, and gain actionable insights. It's a reflective tool to deepen understanding of the strategies discussed in the book. Scan or click the QR below to take this quiz online and receive personalized feedback.

Chapter 6

Emotional Healing and Recovery

Addressing the Root Causes

To truly overcome shopping addiction, it's essential to go beyond the surface and explore the deeper reasons behind your behavior. Compulsive shopping isn't just about wanting more things; it often stems from unresolved emotional, psychological, or even social issues. By addressing these root causes, you can break the cycle of addiction and begin to heal.

One of the most common underlying causes is emotional pain. Many people turn to shopping as a way to cope with difficult emotions like sadness, anxiety, or loneliness. The act of buying something can provide a temporary sense of relief or distraction from the pain, but it never actually resolves the feelings. Over time, shopping becomes a way to numb or escape these emotions. To address this, it's important to identify the emotional triggers that lead to shopping. Once you understand what you're trying to avoid or soothe, you can start to find healthier ways of dealing with those emotions, whether it's through therapy, mindfulness, or self-care practices.

Another significant factor is low self-esteem or insecurity. For some, shopping is a way to improve their self-image or boost confidence. Buying new clothes, accessories, or luxury items can create the illusion of status, success, or attractiveness. However, these external fixes don't address the internal feelings of inadequacy. If you struggle with low self-worth, working on building confidence from within is crucial. This might involve practicing self-compassion, setting personal goals that don't involve material possessions, or surrounding yourself with positive influences that affirm your worth beyond what you own.

Cultural and societal pressures also play a role in shopping addiction. We live in a consumer-driven society that constantly promotes the idea that happiness and success are tied to what we buy. Social media, advertising, and even peer pressure can make it seem like we need the latest trends or gadgets to fit in or feel accomplished. Understanding how these external influences shape your behavior is the first step toward resisting them. Recognizing that your value isn't defined by what you own allows you to step back from the constant push to consume and make more intentional choices about how you spend your money.

Another root cause can be past trauma. For some, shopping becomes a way to regain a sense of control after experiencing trauma or loss. The act of buying something new provides a fleeting feeling of power or comfort, particularly if other areas of life feel overwhelming or out of control. If past trauma is contributing to your shopping habits, seeking professional support from a therapist can help you work through those experiences and develop healthier coping mechanisms.

Finally, habitual behavior can be at the root of shopping addiction. For many, the habit of shopping develops gradually over time, often without realizing it. Whether it's an automatic response to boredom, stress, or an emotional trigger, shopping can become a deeply ingrained behavior. Breaking this habit requires awareness and conscious effort to replace it with more positive actions. This could involve setting new routines, engaging in different activities, or practicing mindfulness to stay present and avoid falling into old patterns.

By addressing these root causes, you can begin to transform your relationship with shopping. It's not just about stopping the behavior but about understanding what drives it, so you can heal from within and create lasting change.

Cognitive Behavioral Techniques (CBT)

CBT is a powerful tool that can help you break free from shopping addiction by addressing the thoughts, emotions, and behaviors that drive your spending habits. The core idea behind CBT is that our thoughts shape our feelings, which in turn influence our actions. By changing the way we think, we can alter how we feel and behave.

One of the first steps in CBT is identifying the thought patterns that lead to impulsive shopping. These thoughts are often automatic and go unnoticed, but they can have a significant impact on your behavior. For example, you might think, "I deserve this" after a hard day or "If I don't buy it now, I'll regret it later." These thoughts can create a sense of urgency or entitlement, making it easier to justify unnecessary purchases. By becoming aware of these thoughts, you can challenge them and replace them with healthier, more balanced thinking.

Once you've identified these unhelpful thoughts, CBT encourages you to reframe them. Instead of thinking, "I deserve this" after a stressful day, you might remind yourself, "I deserve to take care of my long-term financial health." By shifting your mindset, you can begin to see that instant gratification from shopping is not the only way to cope with stress or reward yourself.

Another important aspect of CBT is understanding the emotional triggers that lead to shopping. These emotions can range from stress and anxiety to boredom or loneliness. CBT teaches you to recognize these emotions as they arise and find healthier ways to manage them. For instance, if you tend to shop when you feel anxious, you might try calming activities like deep breathing, meditation, or going for a walk instead of reaching for your phone to shop.

Behavioral experiments are also a key part of CBT. These experiments involve testing out new behaviors to see how they affect your thoughts and feelings. For example, if you're used to buying something as soon as you feel the urge, a behavioral experiment might involve delaying the purchase for 24 hours. During that time, you can observe how the impulse weakens and how your emotions change. This can help you realize that the urgency to shop is often temporary and that you have more control over your actions than you might think.

Another technique in CBT is exposure therapy, which involves gradually confronting situations that trigger your shopping impulses. If going to the mall or browsing online stores is a strong trigger for you, CBT might involve exposing yourself to these situations in a controlled way without making a purchase. Over time, this can reduce the power that these triggers hold, helping you become more comfortable in these environments without giving in to the urge to shop.

Finally, CBT emphasizes building new habits to replace old, unhelpful ones. This might involve setting up new routines that don't involve shopping or finding new ways to reward yourself that don't include spending money. For example, you might develop a habit of treating yourself to a relaxing activity or spending time with loved ones instead of buying something new. These small changes can lead to lasting improvements in your relationship with shopping and your overall well-being.

Cognitive Behavioral Techniques offer practical strategies to help you understand and reshape the thoughts and emotions that drive your shopping habits. By applying these techniques, you can gain greater control over your impulses and build healthier, more sustainable behaviors.

The Role of Therapy and Support Groups

While taking steps to manage your shopping addiction on your own is important, professional support can make a significant difference in your recovery. Therapy and support groups provide structured guidance, emotional support, and tools to help you address the deeper issues behind compulsive spending. They create a space where you can openly discuss your struggles, learn from others, and receive expert advice tailored to your needs.

A therapist can help you explore the underlying emotions and triggers that lead to overspending, offering practical strategies to reframe your thinking and develop healthier habits. Working with a therapist also provides you with a safe, non-judgmental environment where you can openly discuss the challenges you're facing without fear of shame or guilt.

Another benefit of therapy is that it helps you develop emotional regulation skills. Compulsive shopping is often tied to emotional states like stress, anxiety, or sadness. A therapist can guide you in managing these emotions in more constructive ways, helping you to break the link between your feelings and shopping as a coping mechanism. With ongoing support, you can build resilience and learn to handle life's challenges without turning to retail therapy for comfort.

In addition to individual therapy, support groups can be a valuable resource in your journey toward recovery. These groups bring together people who are experiencing similar struggles, offering a sense of community and understanding that can be difficult to find elsewhere. Knowing that you're not alone in your battle with shopping addiction can be incredibly empowering. Support groups allow you to share your experiences, hear from others, and exchange advice on what has worked in managing compulsive spending.

Being part of a support group also helps hold you accountable. Regular meetings encourage you to stay on track with your recovery goals, while the shared experiences of the group provide motivation and inspiration. Support groups are often led by professionals or individuals who have successfully overcome their own addictions, providing guidance that is both practical and relatable.

For many people, therapy and support groups work best when combined. Therapy offers personalized attention and helps you dig deeper into the emotional roots of your addiction, while support groups provide a broader sense of community and shared wisdom. Together, they form a strong foundation for recovery, giving you both the tools and the support system needed to overcome shopping addiction.

Recovery is not a journey that you have to take alone. Therapy and support groups offer a lifeline for those seeking to break free from the cycle of compulsive shopping, providing both the emotional support and practical strategies you need to move forward.

Chapter 7

Long-Term Maintenance and Building Financial Freedom

Staying on Track

Once you've taken the steps to break free from shopping addiction, the challenge becomes staying on track. Change is never easy, and maintaining the progress you've made requires consistent effort and awareness. However, with the right mindset and strategies, you can keep moving forward and prevent old habits from creeping back in.

One of the most effective ways to stay on track is to regularly check in with yourself. Take time to reflect on your emotions, financial goals, and spending habits. Are there times when you feel tempted to return to old behaviors? If so, what's triggering those urges? By staying aware of your emotional state and recognizing patterns, you can address potential issues before they lead to a relapse. Self-awareness is key to long-term success.

Setting clear, achievable goals can also help keep you motivated. These goals don't have to be huge—small wins can be just as important as big milestones. For example, you might aim to go a month without making any unnecessary purchases or work toward saving a certain amount by the end of the year. Each time you reach one of these goals, you'll build more confidence in your ability to manage your spending and make better financial decisions.

It's also helpful to surround yourself with positive influences. This could mean sharing your progress with a trusted friend or family member who can hold you accountable. It could also involve joining online communities or support groups where you can connect with others facing similar challenges. Having people to lean on during tough times can provide encouragement and remind you that you're not alone in this journey.

Additionally, it's important to develop new habits that reinforce your progress. This might involve replacing shopping with healthier activities, such as exercising, pursuing hobbies, or spending time with loved ones. When you feel the urge to shop, try redirecting that energy into something that brings you long-term satisfaction without the financial cost. Over time, these new habits will become a natural part of your routine, making it easier to resist the pull of impulsive shopping.

Regularly reviewing your budget and financial goals is another practical way to stay on track. Tracking your expenses and seeing how far you've come can be incredibly motivating. It also gives you a clear picture of your progress and helps identify any areas where you might need to adjust. Staying on top of your finances allows you to make informed decisions and avoid falling into old spending patterns.

Finally, remember that setbacks are a normal part of any journey. If you slip up, don't be too hard on yourself. What matters most is how you respond. Use the experience as an opportunity to learn and strengthen your resolve moving forward. Staying on track is not about perfection—it's about persistence and continuing to make progress, one step at a time.

Building Healthy Financial Habits

Developing healthy financial habits is a crucial part of overcoming shopping addiction and regaining control over your finances. Just like any other habit, managing money well requires consistency and intentionality. The good news is that by making small, steady changes, you can shift from impulsive spending to responsible financial management. These habits not only help you curb unnecessary spending but also allow you to build a more secure financial future.

One of the most important financial habits to establish is creating and sticking to a budget. A budget helps you keep track of your income and expenses, giving you a clear picture of where your money is going. It allows you to prioritize your spending based on your needs and goals, rather than impulsively buying things you don't need. Start by listing your essential expenses—like rent, utilities, groceries, and debt payments—and then allocate a reasonable amount for discretionary spending. The key is to make sure your spending aligns with your financial goals and doesn't exceed your income.

Another vital habit is saving regularly, even if it's a small amount. Building a savings habit can help you feel more in control of your money and reduce the temptation to spend impulsively. Setting up an automatic transfer from your checking account to a savings account can make this process easier. By saving a portion of your income each month, you can build an emergency fund, save for long-term goals, and have peace of mind knowing you have a financial cushion.

Tracking your spending is also an effective habit for managing your finances. It's easy to lose track of small purchases, but they add up quickly. By keeping a record of every transaction—whether it's using a notebook, an app, or an online tool—you'll become more aware of where your money is going. This awareness makes it easier to identify areas where you can cut back and make more intentional spending choices.

Learning to distinguish between wants and needs is another essential financial habit. Shopping addiction often blurs the line between what's necessary and what's simply desirable. Before making a purchase, ask yourself whether the item is something you truly need or just something you want in the moment. This practice encourages mindfulness in your spending and helps you avoid impulsive purchases.

One way to reinforce healthy financial habits is to set specific financial goals. Whether it's saving for a vacation, paying off debt, or building an emergency fund, having clear goals gives you a sense of purpose and direction with your money. These goals can help you stay focused on the bigger picture and resist the urge to spend on things that don't align with your priorities. Every time you achieve a small goal, like saving a certain amount or paying off a credit card balance, it reinforces your progress and motivates you to keep going.

Finally, developing a habit of financial self-care is crucial. Just as you would take care of your physical and emotional health, your financial health needs attention. This means regularly reviewing your budget, reassessing your goals, and checking in on your spending habits. Financial self-care can also involve learning more about personal finance, whether through reading books, listening to podcasts, or working with a financial advisor. The more informed you are about managing money, the better equipped you'll be to make smart financial decisions.

Building healthy financial habits doesn't happen overnight, but with consistent effort, it becomes easier to manage your money wisely and live within your means. Over time, these habits will become second nature, helping you avoid falling back into impulsive spending and giving you greater confidence in your financial future.

Relapse Prevention

Recovering from shopping addiction is a significant achievement, but maintaining that progress requires ongoing attention and effort. Relapses can happen, especially during times of stress, emotional upheaval, or temptation. The key to preventing relapse is recognizing the signs early and having strategies in place to stay on track.

Relapse Prevention Strategies

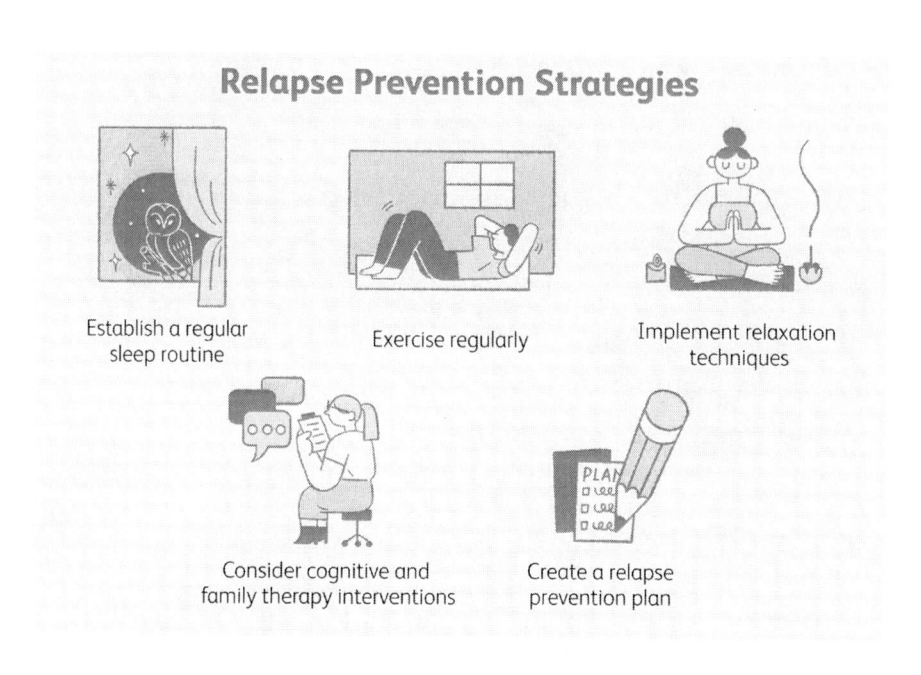

- Establish a regular sleep routine
- Exercise regularly
- Implement relaxation techniques
- Consider cognitive and family therapy interventions
- Create a relapse prevention plan

Relapse Prevention Strategies. Source: verywellhealth.com

The first step in preventing relapse is to understand your triggers. These are the emotional, social, or environmental factors that push you toward impulsive shopping. Perhaps you tend to shop when you're feeling anxious, or maybe browsing online stores has become a way to escape boredom. By identifying your specific triggers, you can be more mindful of situations that put you at risk and develop ways to manage those moments without resorting to shopping.

Another important aspect of relapse prevention is staying connected to your progress. Regularly reflect on how far you've come and the positive changes you've made. Keeping a journal where you track your spending habits, emotions, and goals can be a powerful tool. When you feel the urge to shop, look back at your entries and remind yourself of why you started this journey in the first place. Seeing your progress written down can serve as a strong motivator to keep moving forward.

It's also helpful to establish boundaries that protect you from impulsive buying. This could involve setting specific limits on how much time you spend browsing online or avoiding certain stores that are particularly tempting for you. You can also create a system where you wait at least 24 hours before making any purchase. This delay gives you time to reconsider and helps prevent impulsive decisions.

When cravings to shop arise, it's important to have alternative coping strategies in place. These could be activities that help you relax, distract you, or provide emotional relief. For example, if you feel stressed and are tempted to shop, you might try going for a walk, practicing deep breathing, or engaging in a hobby that brings you joy. Finding non-material ways to soothe your emotions can reduce the need to turn to shopping as a coping mechanism.

A strong support network is also crucial in preventing relapse. Whether it's friends, family members, or a support group, having people you can talk to when you're feeling tempted can make a big difference. They can offer encouragement, hold you accountable, and help you stay grounded during difficult times. Sharing your struggles and victories with others creates a sense of community and helps reinforce your commitment to change.

Finally, it's important to remember that relapse is not the end of your journey. If you do find yourself slipping back into old habits, don't be discouraged. What matters most is how you respond. Take it as a learning experience, identify what triggered the relapse, and use that knowledge to strengthen your defenses moving forward. Progress is rarely a straight line, and setbacks can provide valuable insights into what you need to stay successful in the long run.

Relapse prevention is about staying proactive, remaining mindful of your triggers, and continuing to build habits that support your recovery. With the right tools and mindset, you can maintain the progress you've worked so hard to achieve and avoid slipping back into unhealthy shopping habits.

Chapter 8

The Digital Age and Shopping Addiction

Online Shopping vs. In-Store Shopping

The rise of online shopping has completely transformed the way we buy things. What once required a trip to the store can now be done in seconds from the comfort of your home, often with just a few clicks. While both online and in-store shopping have their advantages and drawbacks, understanding the differences between them is important when managing shopping habits, especially for those struggling with compulsive spending.

One of the biggest advantages of online shopping is its convenience. You can shop anytime, anywhere, without the limitations of store hours or geographical location. This makes it incredibly easy to browse, compare prices, and make purchases. However, this convenience can also be a double-edged sword. The 24/7 accessibility of online shopping makes it harder to resist temptation. The ease of adding items to your cart, often without seeing the money exchange hands, can lead to mindless spending.

Another feature of online shopping is the endless variety of options. With a vast selection of products available from all over the world, it's easy to get overwhelmed or distracted by additional items you didn't plan to buy. Retailers often encourage this by recommending related products or offering free shipping for purchases over a certain amount, which can make it tempting to spend more than intended.

On the other hand, in-store shopping provides a more sensory experience. You can touch, see, and try out products before buying them, which can make the decision-making process feel more grounded. For some, this tactile experience helps reduce the likelihood of impulsive buying, as you can better evaluate whether an item is truly worth the purchase. In-store shopping also tends to have more natural limitations—getting dressed, traveling to the store, and waiting in line—creating barriers that slow down the shopping process, giving you more time to reconsider impulsive purchases.

However, in-store shopping has its own set of challenges. For instance, retailers often use psychological techniques, such as store layouts designed to encourage more browsing or promotional signs that create a sense of urgency. In-store shoppers can also feel pressured by social cues, such as sales associates or other customers, which can lead to impulsive buying decisions.

When it comes to returns and exchanges, online shopping can be less convenient. While purchasing online offers flexibility, returning items often involves packaging the product, printing labels, and mailing it back, which can be a hassle. In-store shopping, on the other hand, allows for quicker returns and exchanges, often on the same day, which can be more convenient for some consumers.

For those dealing with shopping addiction, online shopping may pose more risks. The convenience, anonymity, and instant gratification can make it harder to control spending. It's easy to make impulsive purchases without fully considering the consequences. Online retailers often use targeted ads and personalized recommendations to keep you engaged, making it harder to resist the temptation to buy.

On the other hand, in-store shopping can offer more opportunities to slow down and be mindful of your choices. The physical act of going to a store and interacting with products allows for more deliberate decision-making, which can help curb impulse buying. However, it still requires self-awareness and discipline, especially with tempting sales and promotions right in front of you.

Ultimately, both online and in-store shopping have their pros and cons, but for anyone working to overcome compulsive shopping habits, it's essential to recognize how each environment affects your spending behavior.

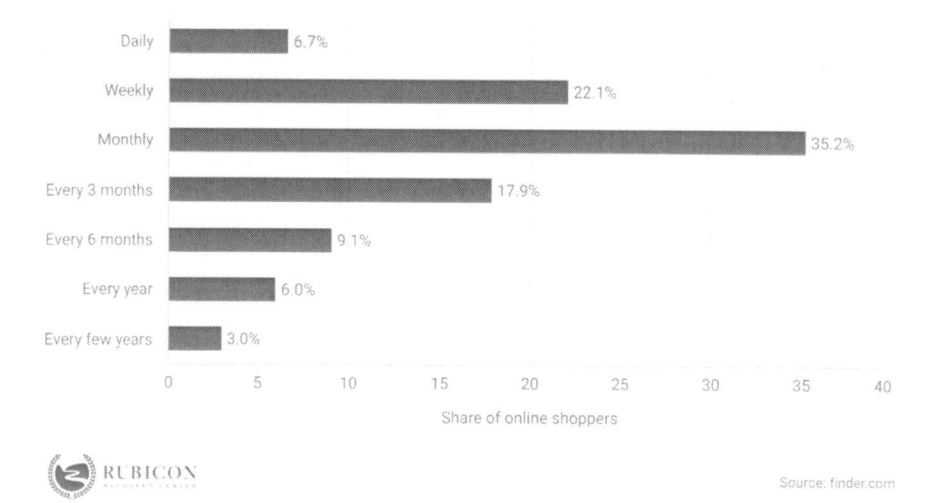

Frequency of Impulsive Online Purchases

Frequency	Share of online shoppers
Daily	6.7%
Weekly	22.1%
Monthly	35.2%
Every 3 months	17.9%
Every 6 months	9.1%
Every year	6.0%
Every few years	3.0%

Source: finder.com

Frequency of Impulsive Online Purchases. Source: rubiconrecoverycenter.com

The Allure of Convenience

In today's fast-paced world, convenience is everything. We can now shop from anywhere, at any time, with just a few taps on our phones or clicks on a computer. The convenience of online shopping has revolutionized how we buy things, making it easier than ever to access a wide range of products without leaving the comfort of home. While this convenience can save time and effort, it also has a downside when it comes to managing spending and avoiding impulsive purchases.

The instant nature of online shopping is one of the biggest draws. With next-day delivery, personalized recommendations, and digital wallets that store your payment information, the entire shopping experience is streamlined to encourage quick decisions. It's tempting to make purchases without fully considering whether you need the item or if it fits into your budget. The sheer ease of buying can lead to overspending before you even realize it.

Another factor that contributes to the allure of convenience is the lack of friction in the buying process. Traditionally, shopping involved more effort—driving to a store, browsing aisles, standing in line, and making payment. All of these steps provided natural pauses that gave you time to rethink your purchases. Online shopping, however, removes these barriers. The process is so seamless that it often feels like you aren't spending real money. This detachment can lead to a false sense of financial security, making it harder to track and control spending.

The convenience of shopping apps also plays a role in reinforcing shopping habits. Many apps send constant notifications about sales, limited-time offers, and personalized deals based on your browsing history. These notifications create a sense of urgency, pushing you to buy now to avoid missing out. With your phone always within reach, it becomes incredibly easy to indulge these impulses, especially during moments of boredom or stress.

The availability of credit is another aspect that fuels the convenience of online shopping. With payment options like "buy now, pay later" services or easy access to credit cards, it's simple to make purchases even when you don't have the funds immediately available. This creates a disconnect between spending and the financial consequences, allowing you to delay the reality of the cost until later, which can quickly add up to significant debt.

Despite these challenges, convenience doesn't have to be a negative force in your life. Being aware of how it affects your shopping habits can help you make more intentional decisions. By introducing small pauses in the process—like removing saved payment information or setting personal spending limits—you can regain control without sacrificing the benefits of convenience. Recognizing the role of convenience in your shopping behavior is a key step in managing your spending and making purchases that truly align with your needs and goals.

Tools to Manage Online Shopping

Online shopping can be convenient, but for those struggling with shopping addiction, it can also be a slippery slope toward overspending. The ease and accessibility of online platforms make it more difficult to resist impulsive purchases. Fortunately, there are several tools and strategies that can help you manage your online shopping habits more effectively, allowing you to stay in control of your spending and make more mindful decisions.

One of the most effective ways to manage online shopping is to set up spending limits. Many banking apps and financial tools offer features that allow you to set daily or monthly spending caps. By defining clear limits on how much you can spend, you create a built-in boundary that helps prevent you from making impulse purchases. Some apps also send notifications when you're approaching your limit, giving you time to pause and rethink any unnecessary buys.

Another useful tool is the use of browser extensions that block or limit access to shopping websites. Extensions like "StayFocusd" or "BlockSite" allow you to restrict the time spent on shopping sites or block them altogether during specific hours. This helps break the cycle of mindless browsing, which often leads to impulsive purchases. If you know that you tend to shop late at night or during certain emotional states, scheduling these sites to be blocked during those times can be an effective strategy.

Shopping cart strategies can also help you manage your online shopping habits. A simple tactic is to leave items in your cart for 24 hours before making a purchase. This waiting period allows you to reconsider whether you truly need or want the item. Often, the initial impulse to buy will fade, and you'll realize that the purchase wasn't necessary after all. Some online stores even send reminders or offer discounts when you leave items in your cart, which may be tempting, but sticking to the 24-hour rule can help you avoid unnecessary spending.

Another helpful tool is the use of price comparison websites and apps. Before making a purchase, take a moment to compare prices across different retailers. This not only ensures that you're getting the best deal but also slows down the decision-making process, allowing you to think more carefully about whether the purchase is worth it. Apps like "Honey" or "CamelCamelCamel" can track price changes and alert you when an item is available at a lower cost, making it easier to avoid impulse buys at full price.

Unsubscribing from promotional emails and turning off notifications from shopping apps is another simple but powerful way to reduce temptation. Retailers often send out daily promotions, flash sales, and exclusive discounts that create a sense of urgency, leading to impulsive purchases. By removing these triggers from your inbox, you create a less tempting environment, making it easier to stay focused on your financial goals.

Finally, using prepaid cards or separate accounts for online shopping can help you stick to a budget. By loading a set amount of money onto a prepaid card or transferring a specific amount into a separate account used solely for shopping, you create a clear limit on how much you can spend. Once the money runs out, it's gone, which prevents you from overspending.

These tools, when combined with mindful shopping practices, can make a significant difference in your ability to manage online shopping. The key is to create boundaries and slow down the process, giving yourself time to make more thoughtful decisions and avoid the trap of impulse buying.

Chapter 9

Success Stories and Lessons Learned

Real-Life Success Stories

Real-life success stories offer hope and inspiration to those struggling with shopping addiction. They show that with the right mindset and tools, it's possible to regain control over your spending habits and rebuild a healthy financial life. Here are a few stories of individuals who managed to overcome their compulsive shopping tendencies, each highlighting the unique challenges they faced and how they found their way to recovery.

Sarah's Story: Finding Balance After Financial Strain

Sarah had always been a self-proclaimed shopaholic. Shopping was her way of rewarding herself after a long workweek, and it became her go-to stress reliever. Over time, Sarah found herself buying more and more things she didn't need, from clothes to home décor. Her credit card debt kept piling up, and she started feeling overwhelmed by the financial strain.

What changed for Sarah was a moment of realization when she could no longer make her minimum payments. She decided it was time to take control of her finances. She started by tracking every purchase, no matter how small, and created a budget that aligned with her true priorities. At first, it was tough, and she experienced withdrawal from not being able to shop as freely as before. But with time, she found new ways to manage her stress, such as going for walks, journaling, and practicing mindfulness.

Sarah's progress didn't happen overnight, but through consistent effort, she paid off her debt and now only shops for things she genuinely needs. The feeling of financial freedom has replaced the temporary rush of buying something new, and she feels more balanced than ever before.

James' Journey: Shifting from Impulse to Intention

James was an impulsive buyer. He didn't think much about his spending, often purchasing items in the heat of the moment, whether it was the latest tech gadget or another pair of sneakers. His impulse shopping led to a growing pile of unused items at home and a dwindling savings account. He began to feel the weight of his decisions when his financial situation became tight, and he realized his lifestyle wasn't sustainable.

Determined to make a change, James started using the 24-hour rule: whenever he felt the urge to buy something, he would wait at least a full day before making the purchase. This simple strategy helped him break the cycle of impulsivity. During that waiting period, he often found that the excitement faded, and he no longer wanted the item as much as he initially thought.

James also became more intentional with his spending, asking himself, "Do I really need this, or is it just a momentary desire?" He focused on saving for bigger goals, like a vacation and building his emergency fund. Over time, James found that his relationship with money had transformed. He now enjoys the satisfaction that comes from thoughtful spending rather than impulsive buying.

Maria's Transformation: Finding Emotional Healing

For Maria, shopping wasn't just a habit—it was an emotional escape. Whenever she felt lonely, stressed, or overwhelmed, she turned to shopping to fill the void. It provided her with a temporary sense of relief, but the relief was always short-lived, and soon the guilt and anxiety would return. Her closet was full of things she didn't need or use, and her financial health was in decline.

Maria realized that in order to break the cycle, she had to address the emotional root of her shopping addiction. She began therapy and learned how to identify and cope with her emotions in healthier ways. Instead of reaching for her credit card when she felt down, she started practicing self-care through exercise, meditation, and spending time with supportive friends.

As Maria worked through her emotional triggers, her compulsive need to shop faded. She gained a deeper sense of fulfillment from activities that truly enriched her life. Today, she no longer views shopping as a way to escape her feelings but as a tool to enhance her life in practical ways when necessary.

These stories reflect the unique paths that different people take toward overcoming shopping addiction. Each individual faced distinct challenges but found success by building self-awareness, creating boundaries, and finding alternative ways to manage their emotions. These real-life examples show that change is possible, and with commitment, anyone can regain control of their spending and live a more fulfilling life.

Lessons from the Journey

The path to overcoming shopping addiction is not a straight line. It is filled with challenges, setbacks, and moments of self-discovery. Along the way, you learn not only how to manage your spending but also deeper lessons about yourself, your emotions, and your relationship with money. These lessons are what ultimately transform your journey from a struggle into a lasting change that benefits every area of your life.

One of the most powerful lessons you'll encounter is the importance of self-awareness. Throughout the journey, you've likely begun to recognize the emotional triggers and patterns that drive your spending. Whether it's stress, boredom, or feelings of inadequacy, understanding these underlying causes is key to long-term recovery. The more aware you are of what fuels your shopping habits, the better equipped you are to manage those feelings in healthier ways.

Another lesson that becomes clear is the value of patience and persistence. Change doesn't happen overnight. There will be moments when you feel like you've taken two steps forward and one step back. But this is part of the process. Building new habits, especially when it comes to managing money and emotions, takes time. What matters is staying committed to the journey and giving yourself grace when you encounter setbacks.

You'll also come to appreciate the power of small victories. It's easy to focus on the bigger goal of financial freedom or being free from shopping addiction, but along the way, you'll find that the small wins are just as important. Each time you resist an impulse purchase, create a budget, or make a mindful financial decision, you're reinforcing new habits. These small victories build momentum, reminding you that progress is possible and that each step counts.

Through this journey, many discover the importance of self-compassion. Often, shopping addiction is tied to feelings of guilt or shame, and it's easy to be hard on yourself for past mistakes. Learning to be kind to yourself, to forgive your past actions, and to focus on what you can control moving forward is a crucial part of healing. Self-compassion allows you to move forward without the burden of guilt holding you back.

Another significant lesson is how stronger boundaries lead to greater freedom. At first, setting limits on your spending or avoiding certain triggers might feel restrictive. But over time, you'll find that these boundaries actually give you more control and freedom in your life. You no longer feel trapped by the constant urge to shop or by financial stress. Instead, you gain the freedom to make intentional choices that align with your values and goals.

Lastly, one of the greatest lessons is that you are not alone. Whether through therapy, support groups, or talking to friends and family, you've learned the value of seeking help and sharing your experiences. Isolation can make addiction feel overwhelming, but reaching out and connecting with others provides the support and accountability needed for lasting change.

Each of these lessons contributes to your growth, not just in managing shopping addiction but in building a healthier, more intentional life. Through this journey, you've gained tools, resilience, and self-understanding that will continue to benefit you far beyond just your spending habits. These lessons are what make the journey worthwhile.

Your Path Forward

Now that you've taken the time to understand shopping addiction, explored practical strategies, and heard real-life success stories, it's time to focus on your path forward. This journey isn't about perfection. It's about progress, awareness, and making consistent choices that support your well-being, both emotionally and financially. Breaking free from shopping addiction is possible, and each step you take brings you closer to that goal.

The most important thing to remember is that change begins with awareness. By recognizing the triggers and emotions that lead you to shop impulsively, you're already taking the first crucial step. Becoming aware of your habits gives you the power to question them, challenge them, and ultimately replace them with healthier behaviors. This self-awareness will serve as your foundation as you move forward.

As you continue on this journey, it's essential to create a plan that works for you. Everyone's experience with shopping addiction is different, and there's no one-size-fits-all solution. Whether it's sticking to a budget, using mindfulness techniques, or developing alternative ways to manage stress, your path should reflect what truly resonates with you and your lifestyle.

Consistency is key. Even small actions, like pausing before making a purchase or tracking your expenses, can have a significant impact over time. These habits, when practiced regularly, will help you stay grounded in your financial goals and keep your impulses in check. The more you build these habits, the easier they will become, and the more control you'll have over your spending.

It's also important to celebrate your victories, no matter how small they may seem. Each time you resist the urge to make an unnecessary purchase, you're proving to yourself that you're capable of change. Acknowledging these successes not only boosts your confidence but also motivates you to keep going, even when the process feels challenging.

Don't hesitate to seek support along the way. Whether it's talking to a friend, joining a support group, or seeking professional help, surrounding yourself with people who understand your journey can make a huge difference. There will be moments when you feel tempted or discouraged, but having a support system can remind you that you're not alone and that your progress is worth the effort.

As you continue on your path, you'll find that the benefits extend far beyond just financial stability. You'll gain a sense of freedom, empowerment, and control over your life. Your relationship with shopping will shift from something that feels overwhelming to something that serves you in a healthy, balanced way. And as you break free from the cycle of impulsive spending, you'll discover new ways to find joy and fulfillment that don't rely on material things.

This path forward is yours to take, and with every step, you're moving closer to a life where your money, your time, and your choices align with the person you want to be.

Conclusion

As we come to the end of this journey, it's important to reflect on the progress you've made and the insights you've gained. Throughout this book, we've explored the complexities of shopping addiction, from understanding the emotional and psychological triggers to developing practical strategies that help you take back control of your finances. You've learned how shopping addiction affects not only your wallet but your mental and emotional well-being as well, and more importantly, how to break free from its grip.

At the heart of this book is the message that shopping addiction is not just about buying things—it's about the deeper emotions that drive those purchases and the habits that form around them. By building self-awareness, creating realistic budgets, and managing your shopping impulses, you have the tools you need to make meaningful changes. Whether you've already started applying these strategies or are just beginning to take the first steps, remember that each action, no matter how small, moves you closer to financial freedom and emotional peace.

The path to overcoming shopping addiction is not always easy, but it's possible. The strategies and techniques discussed in this book are designed to guide you through that process, providing a roadmap for both short-term relief and long-term success. It's about more than just controlling spending—it's about gaining control of your life, your choices, and your future.

As you move forward, carry the lessons you've learned here with you. Be patient with yourself, and remember that change takes time. There will be challenges along the way, but with persistence, self-awareness, and a clear plan, you can overcome the obstacles. You've already taken a brave step by educating yourself and seeking solutions, and that alone speaks to your strength and commitment to change.

Ultimately, this journey is about empowerment—about reclaiming the power you may have once given to shopping and redirecting it toward a more fulfilling, intentional life. You have the ability to rewrite your relationship with money, break free from unhealthy patterns, and create a future that aligns with your values and goals.

Now is the time to take the knowledge you've gained and apply it. The choices you make moving forward are yours to shape, and with the tools in hand, you are more than capable of steering your life in a positive direction. Let this be the beginning of a new chapter—one filled with mindful decisions, financial peace, and a renewed sense of control over your life. The journey ahead is bright, and you have everything you need to move forward with confidence.

Dear Reader,

I hope you found the book insightful and valuable.

Your feedback is invaluable to me. If you enjoyed reading this book, I would appreciate it if you could take a moment to leave a review on the reading apps and platforms.

Thank you for your support, and I wish you all the best.

Kind regards,
Ghazwan

About the Author

Ghazwan is a passionate entrepreneur and business strategist dedicated to helping individuals and organizations achieve their full potential with a deep understanding of modern businesses' challenges and opportunities.

With a Master's degree in Computer and Systems Sciences from Stockholm University, specializing in eService design, requirement engineering, and business process management, he is equipped to innovate cutting-edge solutions.

He believes in the power of collaboration and lifelong learning, and his mission is to empower people to reach their goals and positively impact the world.

Scan or **click** below to connect with him to learn more about his work and stay updated on the latest projects on the following websites:

| ghazwan.pro | LinkedIn | Amazon |

Join our weekly newsletter for exclusive offers, early access to new releases, and other great reads in your inbox.

| OurCommunity |

Manufactured by Amazon.ca
Acheson, AB